Quick
&Easy

The
Well-Behaved
Puppy

D1055862

Dominique De Vito

Quick & Easy
The Well-Behaved Puppy

Project Team
Editor: Heather Russell-Revesz
Copy Editor: Stephanie Fornino
Indexer: Dianne L. Schneider
Cover and interior design: Angela Stanford

T.F.H. Publications
President/CEO: Glen S. Axelrod
Executive Vice President: Mark E. Johnson
Publisher: Christopher T. Reggio
Production Manager: Kathy Bontz

T.F.H. Publications, Inc.
One TFH Plaza
Third and Union Avenues
Neptune City, NJ 07753

10 11 12 13 14   9 11 13 12 10 8
Printed and bound in China

Library of Congress Cataloging-in-Publication Data

De Vito, Dominique.
    The well-behaved puppy : step-by-step techniques for raising a well-adjusted dog / Dominique De Vito.
        p. cm.
    Includes index.
    ISBN 978-0-7938-1004-8 (alk. paper)
    1. Puppies--Training. 2. Dogs--Training. I. Title.
    SF431.D4 2007
    636.7 0887--dc22
                                    2007019785

The Leader in Responsible Animal Care for Over 50 Years!
www.tfh.com

CENTRAL
Garden & Pet

Table of Contents

Quick &Easy

Chapter 1

Bringing Your Puppy Home

From the moment you knew a puppy was for you, you've waited for this moment: bringing your puppy home. After what may have been months of researching breeds to find the one most suitable for your family, visiting breeders, visiting shelters, talking to other dog owners, meeting with family members to discuss responsibilities—finally, finally, today is the day you bring your puppy home. Congratulations! Remember that it's these magical moments that bring real joy to life. Make the day special. Load your camera with film, put a new card in your digital camera, or make sure that the video camera is charged. You'll want to capture these moments and savor them forever. Just remember (as the old saying goes), "Expect the unexpected" when it comes to puppies.

You'll have to do a little preparation before you bring your pup home.

PRE-PUPPY PREP

Before that magical day arrives, you'll need to do a little preparation. Shopping for basic supplies, puppy proofing, and deciding on a schedule should all be completed before your puppy comes home.

BASIC SUPPLIES

One essential part of the preparation process is acquiring the supplies you'll need for your pup. Stick with the items on the checklist and you'll be all set.

Make It Easy: Supplies Checklist

- ☑ baby gate(s)
- ☑ bowls for food and water
- ☑ brush
- ☑ collar
- ☑ cotton bath towels
- ☑ crate
- ☑ crate liner
- ☑ enzymatic cleaner
- ☑ fine-toothed comb
- ☑ first-aid kit
- ☑ identification tag
- ☑ leash
- ☑ nail clippers
- ☑ puppy food
- ☑ puppy treats
- ☑ shampoo
- ☑ toothbrush and toothpaste made for dogs
- ☑ toys

Baby Gate

Finding a functional and even attractive gate to use to confine your puppy is fairly easy these days. There are lots of choices in pet supply catalogs, and you can also find them at pet shops and at places that sell human baby supplies. The gate should be tall and sturdy, able to extend far enough if you have a large opening between rooms, and made of material that won't harm your puppy should he chew on it.

Bowls

Stainless steel and crockery are safe, easy-to-clean choices. Be sure that any stainless bowls you purchase are heavy enough that they won't tip over easily. Puppies are notorious for walking right into their bowls, so solidness is important. Select bowls that are the right size for your puppy—not too big, not too small—and be sure to have separate bowls for water and food.

Did You Know?

Plastic may seem easy to clean and durable, but some claim that it's potentially harmful to dogs. Before you buy, smell it—would you want to eat off some of the plastics being used for dog bowls?

Collar and Leash

There are so many types of collars and leashes on the market that you can have a lot of fun "accessorizing" your pup with colors, patterns, and styles. Before you go crazy getting your puppy different styles for different times of the day or social occasions, though, remember that a puppy is just that: a puppy. He is going to grow—and grow fairly quickly. The first collar and leash combo you should own is one that's practical and comfortable. If your puppy is distracted by the feel or smell of the material, he may develop a habit of trying to paw at or chew the collar and/or the leash.

The ideal first collar for a puppy, whether a toy or giant breed, is a flat buckle collar, preferably made of webbed cotton or nylon. These are simple to get on and off, and they are reliable, washable, and durable.

Make sure that the collar fits properly. One that's too small may choke your pup; one that's too big will come off too easily. Use a tape measure to calculate the circumference of your pup's neck so that you don't have to guess when you get to the store. Once on, you should

Stainless steel bowls are safe and easy to clean.

be able to comfortably fit two fingers between the collar and your pup's neck. Check the size as your pup grows because this could happen faster than you think!

The ideal leash is a 4- to 6-foot-long (1- to 2-m) leash that's also reliable, washable, and durable. Make sure that it's comfortable to hold. It should be long enough to give your pal some space but not so long that the two of you will get tripped up by it as you walk. You may think that a chain leash is fashionable, but it is generally too heavy and difficult to hold comfortably when in use.

Crate and Crate Supplies

There are several styles of crate available, from the functional travel crate that is designed to protect a dog from impact during travel to a soft-sided crate that can serve as a pocketbook so that small dogs can be securely carried by their owners. Folding crates such as those made by Nylabone have the added value and convenience of being easy to store away when not in use. In choosing one that's right for your pup, talk to his breeder about what she uses, and consider how you will want to use the crate yourself. Go to a pet supply store, look through a pet supply catalog, or do some research online to see the many types available and what the pros and cons of each are. Whatever type you choose, buy a crate that is big enough for your puppy to stand up, turn around, and stretch out, but not so big that he can use one

While your puppy might love relaxing on the couch, a crate will keep him safe.

end to eliminate.

Outfit the crate with something soft and warm to lie down on, like a special crate pad or some old towels or blankets. Your pup will appreciate a special toy while he's in the crate —but be sure that it's safe for him to chew on. If you feed your pup in his crate, remove the bowl after he eats. A supply of fresh water can be made available through a drip bottle.

We'll talk about the crate and crate training at length in Chapter 4.

> **Quick Tip**
>
> Having a first-aid kit handy can help to save your puppy's life. You can find a ready-made kit online, or you can assemble your own (see www.canismajor.com/dog/fstaidk.html).

Enzymatic Cleaner

Accidents will happen, and if you don't want your puppy repeating them, you'll need to clean them up quickly and with something that removes the odor. There are numerous enzymatic odor and stain removers on the market to get this job done properly. Be sure to have one handy from the moment you bring your puppy home.

Food and Treats

Hopefully, the person or people from whom you got your puppy told you what they were feeding him and may even have made sure that you had a few days' supply. If possible, keep feeding your puppy whatever it is he's been eating, even if you don't want to keep him on it for more than a week or so. (If that's the case, you'll want to transition foods slowly, as explained in Chapter 2.) If you need a new food right away, select a very high-quality puppy food—the fewer artificial ingredients or preservatives, the better.

As for treats, you'll want items that are gentle on your young pup's system. Don't start tossing him pizza crusts or other table scraps. Do have some nutritious, size-appropriate puppy "cookies" for him. These will help clean his teeth while satisfying his hunger and need to chew.

Grooming Supplies

Depending on your puppy's breed, grooming can become quite complicated. You can learn about his particular needs by reading a breed-specific book, but most puppies will need a soft bristle brush, a fine-toothed comb, a puppy-appropriate shampoo, nail clippers, toothbrush (or gauze pads) and toothpaste made for dogs, and towels.

Learn more about grooming in Chapter 2.

An ID tag can help to identify your pup if he ever gets lost.

ID Tag

Your pup's identification tag is something he could find really distracting if it's too shiny or large. While he's growing, go with the smallest tag that's practical for his size, and keep it simple. Include your dog's name and your phone number on the tag.

Toys

Shopping for doggy toys is so much fun! Toys come in all shapes and sizes, make funny noises, can be interactive, and much more. Before selecting what you think is cute, think about your dog. His size is going to influence your choice, and so is his potential for chewing. Some puppies just nibble at things; some puppies shred even the toughest materials. Leading manufacturers, such as Nylabone, include safety sheets with their chews and toys to help puppy parents select appropriate items. Follow their suggestions, and monitor your puppy while he's playing. You don't want him to chew off and swallow large pieces of anything, or the squeakers that come in some toys.

SETTING UP A SCHEDULE

A word to the wise: Figure out a practical, doable schedule to feed, exercise, walk, and play with your puppy before you bring him home. Why? Because you'll want to start using it right away. Puppies, like children, thrive on routine. Your puppy will be better behaved and more manageable if you can put him on a schedule and stick to it. You will understand why just a few short weeks into your puppy-owning experience.

Puppies are fairly predictable. They need to eat, sleep, be taken outside or to a designated spot to relieve themselves, go for walks and participate in other forms of exercise, and interact with other members of the family. The primary influences on your schedule will be when the puppy goes outside or to his designated spot, and when he eats. These

Make It Easy: Puppy Proofing

Before introducing him to your new home, take a look at your home from your puppy's point of view. Secure anything that is potentially dangerous, or put it out of his reach. This includes medicines, household cleaners, electric cords, certain houseplants, small objects like buttons or kids' toys with removable parts that can be easily swallowed, and so on. Some puppies develop a fascination for toilet paper or tissues. While not particularly harmful, walking into a room full of shredded toilet paper or tissues is annoying, and it's a habit you want to keep your pup from getting into from the beginning. Keep toilet paper rolls rolled up, and place tissue boxes out of reach.

things will depend partly on his age and partly on his temperament. Some puppies get the housetraining thing down quickly and easily, and some do not. Chapter 4 is all about housetraining, so be sure to study it. But for now, let's look at how feeding and housetraining fit into your puppy's day.

Eight- to Twelve-Week-Old Pups

Young puppies need to go outside or "do their business" as soon as they get up in the morning, so be ready! If your bundle of fluff wakes you at 6:00 a.m. whining and possibly circling, it's time to get him out. Do not expect a young puppy to adjust to your normal time of getting up; for now, you'll need to take care of him first.

After relieving himself, your puppy will be hungry. Then he'll want to play, and he'll need to go outside again soon after eating. See the chart on page 12 for a typical schedule for a family that is gone most of the day.

If this seems like a lot of work, it is! However, the better able you are to stick to this kind of schedule, the

Quick Tip

Select toys and chews that are size and chew-strength appropriate for your puppy.

more quickly your puppy will be housetrained, and the faster you'll find him settling into the family routine. If getting home to care for the puppy around midday is impossible for you, find and set up an arrangement with a local pet-sitting or pet-walking service to come in and take care of your puppy. It is inhumane to leave a young puppy (or even an older dog) alone for more than a few hours at a time, and you certainly can't expect a baby puppy not to have accidents in the

A Typical Schedule for Your Puppy

6:00 a.m.	Take puppy out to relieve himself.
6:15 a.m.	Feed first meal.
6:30–6:45 a.m.	Play with puppy.
6:45 a.m.	Take puppy back outside to relieve himself.
7:00 a.m.	Confine puppy while taking care of self/children.
7:30/8:00 a.m.	Take puppy out.
8:00 a.m.	Crate or confine puppy while you/you and children are gone.
11:30/Noon	Take puppy out to relieve himself.
Noon	Feed puppy second meal.
12:15 p.m.	Take puppy back outside to relieve himself.
12:30 p.m.	Confine puppy if leaving the house again.
3:00 p.m.	Take puppy out when children are home from school.
3:15 p.m.	Feed puppy a nutritious snack.
3:30 p.m.	Take puppy out again.
3:45–5:00 p.m.	Interact with puppy as appropriate. This is a good time for some basic training, socializing, going for walks around the neighborhood, playing, or supervised time in the rest of the house. Take time for potty breaks.
5:30 p.m.	Take puppy out, then feed third meal.
5:45 p.m.	Take puppy out again.
6:00–8:00 p.m.	Supervised play/exercise/training time with family.
Before your bedtime	Take puppy out.
At bedtime	Confine puppy to sleeping area.

house if he can't get out to relieve himself.

THE BIG DAY

Whether your new puppy is arriving via airplane from a breeder who lives across the country, or whether you fell in love with a shelter pup and just had to bring him home that instant, you're bound to experience that transitional time of bringing your pup from his first home to his forever home.

THE CAR RIDE

Bring the following items with you to pick up your puppy: collar, leash, travel crate, clean towels, and paper towels. You will be tempted to hold the pup in your lap on the ride home, but the safest place for him is in the crate in the backseat. You (or a family member or friend) should sit in the back with him to speak nicely to him or to quiet him should he get upset. The towel may come in handy if he has an accident, and the paper towels are for backup. Don't feed the pup during the trip, even if it's several hours long. This may upset his stomach. A plush toy may help to keep him company in the crate, but your presence is the best thing.

THE FIRST NIGHT

My goodness, what a day for all of you when your puppy finally comes home! By bedtime you will all be excited and tired. Plan to have a low-key evening at home the first few nights your puppy is with you. No dinner parties or late-night teenager get-togethers—and cancel any plans you've made to go out. Your puppy needs you on his first night away from his mom and siblings.

After dinner and potty/play time, you can have your puppy join you for whatever after-dinner activities you had in mind, whether it's playing a game, reading, or watching television. If your puppy seems energetic and playful, much of your evening may be spent entertaining him. If he's sleepy, you can let him rest in your lap or next to you on the sofa. Let his energy level determine how involved you are with him.

When you're ready to go to bed, take the puppy out to relieve himself one last time, even if you have to wake him up to do it. If you're crate training your puppy (more on that in Chapter 4), put him in his crate for the night. Even if you eventually want your

Quick Tip

Pack your new puppy's collar and leash, travel crate, and some old, clean towels and paper towels into the car the night before you pick him up so that you don't forget anything in your excitement.

Your puppy might be frightened at first—don't let friends and family overwhelm him.

dog to sleep in the kitchen and not in one of your bedrooms, all of you will sleep better the first night if you bring him into your room (not one of the kids' rooms, no matter how much they plead). Put the crate somewhere where your puppy can see and hear you.

Things That Go Yip in the Night

Your puppy may whine, yip, or even bark or howl during the night. No matter how pitiful he sounds, don't take him out of the crate and put him in your bed unless you want to do this for possibly the rest of his life. Besides allowing him to come up and sleep on your bed, you're giving him the message that you and he are equals; after all, the only other living beings he slept with were his doggy mom and siblings. From your puppy's perspective, he will have simply traded up in size.

If your puppy is vocalizing during the night, you can say "Shush" to him, or even tap on the crate while saying "Shush." If he stops, let him know you're happy by saying "Good puppy." If he continues to make noise, do your best to ignore him. If he wakes up in the middle of the night crying, he may need to go outside. Take him, no matter how hard it is for you to get out of bed. If he relieves himself, let him know he's a good boy, and then get him straight back to bed. You'll have

Bringing Your Puppy Home

to make the call whether you think your puppy needs to go out or whether he's just lonely. You don't want him to think that every time he makes a fuss you're going to get up and take him out, but you also don't want him to soil his bed because you couldn't be bothered. Be prepared for some fitful nights the first week or so as your puppy acclimates to his new home. This, too, shall pass!

WELCOME TO THE FAMILY: KIDS AND YOUR PUPPY

It is your responsibility to ensure that the puppy is treated kindly and safely by your children (and their friends).

Before you bring your puppy home, review his schedule with the whole family. Assign particular feeding and "taking out" times to children who are old enough for this responsibility. Talk about how important it is to care for the puppy properly.

Once your puppy is home, let each child spend some one-on-one time with him (under adult supervision, of course). Confine the interaction to one room of the house in case the puppy does have an accident. A room with a floor that's easy to clean is your best bet, whether it's a "mud" room, kitchen, or bathroom. Ask the child to sit on the floor to play with the puppy so that if the puppy slips from her grasp, he won't fall far. Explain how to hold the puppy properly—with his full body supported from underneath—and otherwise just let them be with each other.

Puppies have sharp teeth and use their mouths to explore their world. Should the puppy play-bite anyone in the family, let him know that this is unacceptable by immediately making a loud crying noise as a hurt dog would. This will startle the puppy so that he'll stop mouthing and look at you. Have a suitable chew toy ready to give him, and tell him what a good boy he is to chew on it instead.

Once your children have each had time with the puppy by themselves, let them play together. For the first week or so, keep playtime as quiet as possible. Children and puppies can get rowdy quickly, leading to rough play and a greater chance of getting hurt. Don't let this happen to your children or the puppy; it could damage how they feel about each other for a long time.

Quick Tip

The child-puppy dynamic is a fascinating one and is more complicated (and interesting) than this book has time for. To learn more, read *Raising Puppies & Kids Together: A Guide for Parents*, by Pia Silvani and Lynn Eckhardt.

15

Chapter 2

Taking Care of Your Puppy:
Feeding and Grooming

You're now the meal planner for another member of the household! Unlike a child who, as he grows, can learn to take care of himself, your puppy is going to need you to make the decisions about what and how much he'll eat for his entire life.

There's a saying that good health starts from the inside out, and that's certainly the case with dogs. If they eat junk, they'll look, smell, and feel bad. If they eat a nutritionally sound diet, their coats will shine, their eyes will sparkle, and their energy level will be normal. Of course, a sound diet goes hand in hand with regular grooming and sufficient exercise for a dog who exudes good health.

How much you feed your pup depends on his size and appetite.

FEEDING YOUR PUPPY

If you acquired your puppy from a reputable breeder or otherwise conscientious source, he probably came with a week's supply of whatever he was being fed, along with specific instructions for when and how much of the food to feed, and when to switch meal plans. If not, don't worry; this book will help you learn what to do.

WHAT TO FEED

The first thing you want to do is have a supply of top-quality puppy food. Whether you choose dry, canned, or a combination of the two, don't economize in this area—although it may seem tempting with all the selections that are available. If studying dog food labels isn't what you have time for right now, get advice from someone you trust, like a friend whose dogs look healthy to you, the veterinarian you'll be taking your puppy to, a breeder, or even a local trainer.

Quick Tip

If you're uncertain whether you're feeding your pup too much or too little food, consult your veterinarian.

WHEN TO FEED

When your puppy is 4 months (16 weeks) old or younger, he should be eating four times a day. This is because his stomach is small and his metabolism is high. Don't try to cram the four meals into two meals. This can lead to an upset stomach from overeating, then hunger from not eating.

Review the sample schedule outlined in Chapter 1. Your puppy's first meal should be just after he is taken outside to relieve himself first thing in the morning, and he should be fed every four hours or so afterward, with his last meal coming around 6:00 or 7:00 p.m. The third meal of the day can be a "snack"—a couple of puppy biscuits, some peeled baby carrots, or some lean cooked meat and oatmeal—the snack can vary as long as it's good for your puppy. Feeding a snack from your hands (or having your kids or friends do it) helps the puppy learn that all different people are the source of yummy things.

HOW MUCH TO FEED

How much you feed your puppy depends on his size and appetite. Your pup's previous owner should give you an idea of how much your puppy was eating, but if she didn't, you'll need to experiment to find the ideal quantity. You don't want to overfeed, but neither do you want to underfeed. Small puppies can start on approximately 1/2 cup (113 g) of dry food per meal, while larger pups may eat up to 1 cup (227 g) at each meal. Determine the ideal quantity by assessing your pup's overall appetite and appearance. If he's gobbling up the food in seconds and wants more, add some. If he doesn't finish his portion, consider cutting back.

Always have fresh water available for your dog.

Don't let your puppy become too much of a butterball. An overly chubby puppy may look cute, but the extra weight isn't good for him. On the other hand, puppies need some baby fat, so don't think that your dog needs to look like the tucked, fit adults

 **Quick Tip**

Hand-feed your pup his snack so that he learns to take food nicely; use the food to teach and reinforce basic requests like sit, down, come, stay, off, wait, and much more. (See Chapter 5 for more on training.)

of his breed. Furry puppies can be more difficult to gauge for proper weight.

NO FREE-FEEDING

You may be tempted to put a bowl of food down for your pup and leave him to finish it when he so chooses, a method called free-feeding. This isn't a good idea for several reasons. The first is your puppy's health. A poor appetite can be one of the first signs that something is wrong with your dog. While your puppy may not be overly enthusiastic about every meal, he should certainly be eager to eat and should finish the (reasonable) amount of food you put in his bowl for the allocated meal. If that's not happening, take him to the veterinarian.

Another reason free-feeding is detrimental is that it teaches your dog that food is available almost any time. Because food can (and should) be a major motivator for your dog, you can use it to develop a better relationship with him through training and sharing.

Make sure that the snacks you feed your puppy are healthy.

THE FEEDING ROUTINE

At each meal, prepare your puppy's food and put it in his designated eating spot. Leave the bowl for no longer than 15 minutes. If your puppy hasn't eaten everything, don't worry. Pick the bowl up, discard the uneaten food, clean the bowl, provide fresh water, and consider mealtime over. Go through the same routine for every meal.

Your puppy depends on you to find him a healthy diet.

MEALTIME MANNERS

Mealtime is a great time to teach your puppy manners that will make him an appreciated member of the family as he grows. The first is to sit for dinner. Using the lessons in Chapter 5 to teach *sit* and *stay*, ask your puppy to do these two things before every meal. When he's very young, he can do a quick *sit-stay* as you are about to put his food bowl down. As he gets older, ask him to sit and then stay as you prepare his food, allowing him to come and get it only when the bowl is on the floor. He'll learn quickly that he gets rewarded with food for doing a great *sit-stay*.

YOUR GROWING PUPPY'S NUTRITIONAL NEEDS

From the ages of 4 to 8 months (16 to 32 weeks), you can reduce your pup's meals to two regular meals and one healthy snack, and at about 8 months, consider switching to a maintenance formula rather than a puppy formula. If you're unsure about when to make the switch, consult a trusted source like your puppy's breeder, veterinarian, or trainer.

Dogs are considered puppies through their "adolescence"—some time between 12 and 18 months, depending on the breed and the individual dog. Especially if your dog is active, there is no need to cut

back on the amount you're feeding him as long as he is in good health. Your veterinarian can advise on whether your pup is getting too much or too little food.

GROOMING YOUR PUPPY

While good health and good looks certainly start from the inside, tending to your pup's appearance is essential as well. You will need to groom your dog all over, from the tip of his nose to the tips of his paws to the tip of his tail. That means brushing him, bathing him, tending to his eyes, ears, nails, and bottom, and maintaining his oral health.

WHERE TO GROOM

If you have a pup who needs more attention to grooming, like a double-coated breed or a terrier, you may want to invest in a grooming table. It can be folded up when you're not using it, and it is specially designed to allow your puppy or dog to stand or lie down on it while on a leash, letting you use both hands to tend to him. A grooming table is covered with nonskid soft rubber—an ideal surface to work on.

If you don't want to buy a grooming table, designate a spot in the house where you can groom your dog regularly. Put your grooming supplies in a single container so that they are readily available to you when you need them. Put your puppy's collar and leash on so that you have some control over him, and stand him on the floor or place a towel on the floor under you. Put some small, easy-to-eat treats in a container next to you.

GETTING YOUR PUPPY USED TO GROOMING

You and your pup should consider grooming time enjoyable and look forward to it. A pup who bites at brushes and combs or who won't be still while you examine his feet or mouth is also a pup who may give the veterinarian a hard time when it comes to examining him for his health. This could lead to your veterinarian needing to muzzle your dog just to check him out, which is unpleasant for everyone.

Make It Easy: Grooming Supplies

Here are the supplies you'll need to make grooming your puppy a snap:
- brush (type will vary depending on your breed's coat type)
- comb
- cotton balls
- dog shampoo
- dog toothbrush and dog toothpaste
- gauze pad
- grooming table (optional)
- nail clippers
- plastic container (for rinsing)
- styptic pen or powder
- towels

It can be helpful to keep all your supplies in a container for easy access.

Don't expect your pup to take to grooming instantly; rather, teach him to enjoy it. You should start as soon as you bring him home. Have some tasty treats handy, and begin touching your puppy all over his body. Reward him with a treat when he stays calm. Touch his feet, belly, tail, and head. Go slowly at first—try using a treat held near his nose to distract him, and examine an ear. Do the same as you check the other ear. Run your hands over your pup to check for any skin abnormalities. That's enough for one day! Increase the length and amount of grooming you do with your pup day by day as you use the treats.

BRUSHING

Your puppy will inevitably find grooming tools chew-worthy. Distract him from playing with or chewing the brush by holding a treat in your hand and letting him sniff at it without getting it.

How to Brush Your Puppy

Using a brush that's appropriate for the length of your dog's fur, begin at the head and work your way back to the body, legs, and tail, brushing in the direction of the hair growth to remove loose and dead hair. If your dog has extra feathering around his ears, on his legs, or under his tail, use a comb to work through this finer fur.

When you've gone from head to tail, give your puppy a treat.

BATHING

Just like your grooming routine, you'll want to acclimate your puppy to being bathed by going slowly and gently and rewarding him for good behavior.

Getting Started

Because most puppies are small enough to fit in a sink or bathtub, getting started is fairly easy. Put a rubber mat in the sink or tub for traction, and keep your pup's collar on for extra control.

As the water is running to warm up, make a fuss over the sink or tub to show how positively you feel about this.

Bathing will keep your pup looking and feeling good.

Make It Easy: Grooming Routine

Eventually, you'll want to establish a grooming routine. Here's the checklist:

- Brush the entire body.
- Comb where necessary.
- Examine ears, eyes, nose, and mouth.
- Keep the nails trimmed.
- Keep the anus clear of matted fur or waste buildup.

If you make a point of going over your pup this way at least once a week, he will radiate good health.

Give your pup a couple of treats for being near you while you're waiting for the water to get warm. (Never put your pup in the wash receptacle and then turn the water on.) While you're waiting for the bathwater to warm up, gather your supplies: shampoo, a plastic container to use for rinsing, and a few clean, dry towels.

When everything is ready, bend down to pick up your puppy and offer him a very tasty treat. Scoop him up in your arms and close the bathroom door if you're using the tub (so that he can't make a great escape).

How to Bathe Your Puppy

With the warm water running gently, put your pup in the wash basin and hold him under his belly or by his collar. Put a cotton ball in each ear if you can to keep water from running into them. Begin wetting him with water from the container—don't push him under the faucet. Speak reassuringly to him as you get him wet. Very few dogs enjoy being bathed, so expect your pup to struggle a bit.

Once he's wet all over, apply shampoo along his back from his neck down. Wash his neck and the top of his head with the lather from his back because you want to keep the shampoo away from his eyes, nose, and ears as much as possible. Work the shampoo into a lather on his body and down his legs, being sure to get some on his tummy and between his legs, too.

Quick Tip

Brush your puppy before bathing him. Any mats or knotted fur will only get worse when wet.

Don't forget to wash his tail.

When you've scrubbed him all over, begin to rinse, again applying warm water from the container, not from the faucet. Rinse thoroughly, then rinse again. You want to remove all soapy residue from the fur. Use a wet washcloth to clean around your pup's face.

Getting Dry

When he's rinsed, turn the water off and begin drying him with a towel. Let him shake himself, but hold on to him so that he doesn't jump out of the sink or tub. Towel dry him as well as you can, and go over him quickly with a soft brush. Then let him loose, and look out.

EARS, EYES, AND NOSE

Examine your puppy's ears, eyes, nose, and mouth. Use a moist cotton ball to wipe away any crust or gunk around the eyes and nose. Inspect the ears for any odor or waxy buildup. Remove what you can with a moist cotton ball, but don't put anything deeply into the ear.

CLIPPING NAILS

Nail clipping is the biggest grooming challenge most dog owners face, and it's no wonder! If you cut too much of the nail off, you hit the quick (the blood vessel that runs through the nail), causing your pup pain and the nail to bleed. This is no fun for anyone! But if you don't cut enough of the nail off, you'll have to do it again soon. Meanwhile, puppies tend to have sensitive paws, squirming and biting as you hold them to try to get to the nail, making the whole process more difficult. And yet it's essential that dogs' nails stay trimmed because nails that are too long can cause your pup's feet to splay as they grow; the nails can even curl under and grow into the pad. What to do?

Get your puppy used to nail trimming right away.

The earlier you get your puppy used to grooming, the easier it will be for both of you.

How to Trim Your Puppy's Nails

Again, slow and steady wins the race. First show the nail clippers to your pup, and give him a treat while he sniffs them. Hold them near his feet without touching his paws, and give him another treat. Spend a few days just acclimating your pup to the nail trimmers before trying to trim all the nails in one session.

When you're ready, position yourself and him so that you can comfortably clip his nails. If you groom your dog on a table, just stand by him as you do when brushing him. If you groom your pup "on the fly," as the mood strikes, the best position is probably sitting or kneeling beside him so that you can hold him should he squirm. With him mouthing at a treat in one of your hands, try to discreetly position just the tip of a nail in the trimmer, and snip it off as you give the treat. How do you know if you have the nail trimmer positioned in the correct spot? For pups with white nails, it's easier to see where the quick starts—it looks pinkish in the nail. You can't see this in a black nail. Err on the side of caution, and position the nail trimmer so that there is just a tiny bit of nail in it.

If you accidentally clip into the quick, put a tissue or gauze pad against the nail to stem the bleeding, and apply styptic powder or soap to stop the bleeding. You will need to return to the task another day because your puppy will be uncomfortable.

It is often easier to have a friend or family member help with nail trimming. This way, one person can keep the pup distracted with a treat while the other does the holding and clipping. If you're too nervous to do it yourself, ask your veterinarian or a groomer to show you how.

DOGGY DENTAL CARE

What would your mouth look and feel like if you never brushed your teeth? Not a pleasant thought. Dogs don't care as much as we do about the look and feel of their mouths, but certainly the health effects of inattention are undeniable. Plaque and tartar lead to periodontal disease, which is potentially life threatening.

How to Brush Your Puppy's Teeth

An ounce of prevention is definitely worth a pound of cure. While you're getting your puppy used to being groomed and handled, including inspecting his mouth, you can introduce him to doggy toothpaste by putting a dab on your finger and rubbing it over his teeth. Over the course of a month or so, continue to increase the time and pressure you spend on the mouth, putting the toothpaste on a gauze pad and rubbing it into the teeth and gums. When your pup is used to the process, introduce a doggy toothbrush to help you get the job done.

Veterinarians would like us to brush our dogs' teeth every day. If you can't manage that, try to do it as often as possible.

Another way to keep your dog's teeth, jaws, and mouth healthy is to provide proper chews, as discussed in the feeding section of this chapter. Chews help to reduce and remove plaque and tartar buildup, as well as exercise the jaws.

Did You Know?

The "quick" is the blood vessel that runs down the center of your dog's toenails.

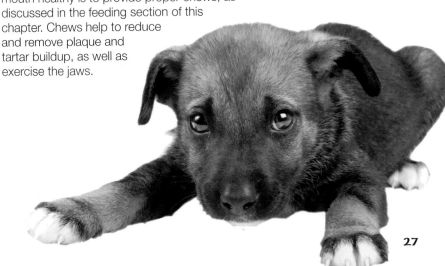

Quick &Easy

Chapter 3

Keeping Your Puppy Healthy

Because you and your veterinarian will be working together to keep your pup healthy, finding someone you feel comfortable with is important. Hopefully, you'll have time to find the right vet before you bring your puppy home. He will need to see a veterinarian within the first few days of being with you so that he can get a thorough checkup; leaving this critical visit to a vet you don't know is not in your pup's best interest.

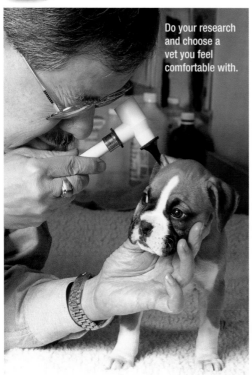

Do your research and choose a vet you feel comfortable with.

CHOOSING A VETERINARIAN

If you're acquiring your puppy locally, ask your puppy's breeder for a referral. Ask friend and neighbors for suggestions. Look in the yellow pages for listings of veterinarians in the area, and make a point to visit them.

When you go to a vet's office, take note of the following:
• Are the receptionists pleasant and helpful?
• Is the waiting room crowded?
• Do the people and their animals seem comfortable there?
• Is the facility overly noisy, smelly, or dirty?

Call ahead to make an appointment with the head of the practice, and when you meet, feel free to ask her about vaccinations, emergency care, nutrition—whatever your concerns may be. Let the vet know when you're getting your puppy, and see what advice she has for you. The vet should be eager to get you and your puppy off on the right paw to wellness.

YOUR PUPPY'S FIRST VET VISIT

Schedule your pup's first appointment ahead of time. When you go in, remember to take a fresh stool sample. The veterinarian's lab will examine it under a microscope for the presence of parasites. At your first appointment, your veterinarian will want to be sure that your puppy is in overall good health. She will give your puppy a thorough going-over, beginning at the pup's head and going all the way to his tail.

When the full physical examination is over, your vet will review your puppy's schedule for vaccinations.

VACCINATIONS

Puppies need vaccinations so that they don't acquire life-threatening contagious diseases like distemper, leptospirosis, rabies, and the like. Recently, there has been considerable debate in the animal health community about the strength, combinations, and timing of the routine vaccinations given to pets. This is something you should research further, discuss with your veterinarian, and come to a personal decision about. For your individual dog, the vaccination schedule that's been in place in the veterinary community for decades may need tweaking.

Regardless of how you and your veterinarian decide to approach the issue of vaccinations, the fact is that your puppy does need them. A typical vaccination schedule begins when your puppy is about six weeks of age, continues every three to four weeks until all shots are given, and then proceeds annually or as you and your vet decide. The diseases your pup will be vaccinated against at this age are distemper, hepatitis, leptospirosis, parvovirus, and parainfluenza. When he's old enough, your pup will also need a rabies vaccine, and depending on where you live, one for Lyme disease. He'll also need one for bordetella, or kennel cough, if he will be around strange dogs frequently (for example, at a kennel or a dog show).

Your veterinarian will put your puppy on a schedule to receive his full round of shots. Stick to the schedule so that you don't risk compromising your pup's health. Also, the sooner he's "covered," the sooner he can get out into the world and start really socializing.

Quick Tip

Don't be a stranger to your veterinarian. Remember that she is there as a resource for you at all times. As your puppy grows, you will need to bring him in to see the vet at least once a year.

Vaccinations have saved the lives of millions of dogs.

Spaying or neutering is good for your dog's health.

Spaying or Neutering Your Puppy

Spaying is the removal of a female dog's reproductive organs; neutering is the removal of the male's testicles. The objective is to eliminate your dog's reproductive capacity. Why is this important for you and your pet?

- **Health:** Your dog won't suffer a disease of his or her reproductive organs.
- **Behavior:** Your female won't come into heat and attract males, and your male won't have the desire to find females. Also, spaying or neutering tends to dampen territorial responses and aggressive tendencies.
- **Overpopulation:** There are far too many puppies and dogs without homes. Only the most conscientious of breeders should consider producing more animals.

The procedure is simple and safe, so don't put it off.

Bug Off! Fleas, Ticks, and Other Pests

Creepy crawly bugs have been making dogs' lives

miserable for centuries. Our companions depend on us to help to keep them as pest-free as possible, and fortunately, there are a lot of ways to do that these days. Another great thing is that pest management for our pets is becoming less toxic over time, too. The important things are to be informed and to follow the instructions of the products you decide to use.

FLEAS ARE NOT FRIENDS

Flea bites cause more than annoying itching—they can lead to tapeworm infections and flea-bite allergies that can plague a pet for life. Fleas also bite people.

Preventing Fleas

Prevention is your best tactic in the war against fleas. It is believed that fleas and other pests prey on animals (and people) with compromised immune systems, and it's true that if your body can't fight off the effect of whatever is attacking it, that predator has found a home.

The first thing to do is to review what you're feeding your puppy. A month or so before peak flea season in your area, consider supplementing his diet with nutrients that ramp up the immune system. Discuss this with your veterinarian before you begin supplementing.

The second thing to do is to be fastidious with your grooming. After every significant trip outdoors, go over your dog, inspecting his fur closely and even running a fine-toothed flea comb through his coat. Pay special attention to areas that fleas tend to like—behind the ears, between the legs, and above the tail. When you see a flea, try to crush it either between your fingers or against the handle of the flea comb. Dabbing on rubbing alcohol or hydrogen peroxide on the flea will numb it so that you can really grab it.

The third thing to do is to keep your house and grounds as clean as possible. Vacuum thoroughly; clean dog beds weekly; rake and keep clear any outdoor sleeping areas your dog frequents. You want to eliminate any potential breeding ground for fleas.

You should also discuss with your veterinarian using one of the many products on the market that have been developed to kill fleas on an animal before they can settle in and start feeding or breeding. These include products that can be ingested, as

Quick Tip

Keep your flea inspection and removal materials near the door where you and your dog go in and out, and make it a habit to inspect your dog after each outing.

Inspect your puppy for fleas after he's been outside.

well as those that can be applied to the skin. It's important to choose what can be most effective but also least toxic to your puppy, and that might depend on any number of things, from breed type to where you live.

Getting Rid of Fleas

If, despite these preventive measures, you develop a flea problem, you will need a plan to eliminate each life stage of the beasts.

First, get the fleas off your animal(s) by combing with a flea comb, then bathing with a flea-killing or preventive shampoo. Beware the toxic ingredients in a flea-killing shampoo or dip, and follow up with something restorative and healing for the skin. Comb every day, and bathe as necessary.

Second, remove the various life stages from the environment. Eggs, larvae, and pupae could be anywhere your pet has been in the house and yard. Wash his dog beds and any sheets or blankets he has slept on in very hot water. Double rinse! Vacuum everywhere, carefully removing the vacuum bag after doing so. Put the vacuum bag in a plastic bag, and seal it securely before disposing of it permanently.

Talk to your veterinarian and pet supply store personnel about the products available to assist in removing fleas from your home and yard. There are special powders and sprays you can use, but it's important to understand what they do and of course to follow the instructions for their use to the letter.

TICKS ARE TERRIBLE

Ticks cause problems. There are small, clingy ones that can cause Rocky Mountain spotted fever and gray ones that expand as they fill with blood. Plus, many parts of the US need to worry about the Lyme disease tick—one that's so small you can mistake it for a freckle or speck of pepper, and so deadly it can lead to severe arthritis.

How can you keep yourself and your puppy safe from these predators?

Preventing and Getting Rid of Ticks

The preventive measures outlined for keeping fleas at bay also work for ticks. As time consuming and annoying as it may be, a thorough inspection of your pup's entire body as soon as he comes in from being outside is critical. This is your best chance to nab the bugs before they can bite your dog or settle in your house.

Removing Ticks From Your Puppy

If you're lucky, you'll catch these tiny monsters before they bite your puppy (or you). If you find a tick attached to your dog, remove the entire tick. If the head stays attached, it can cause infection. Numb the tick by dabbing it with rubbing alcohol or hydrogen peroxide, and use tweezers to grab the tick as close to the skin as possible. Carefully pry the tick off your pup; don't pull or grab too quickly. To be sure that the tick can't come after you again, drown it in soapy water or flush it down the toilet. Yuck!

Apply antibiotic ointment to the bite wound, being sure to rub it in. Reapply every few hours, and keep an eye on the wound. If it swells or appears to be aggravating your puppy, call your veterinarian.

Make It Easy: Dealing with Emergencies

The Boy Scouts' advice about being prepared is apt when you're dealing with an emergency. Before an emergency strikes, take the following precautions:

- Post your veterinary clinic's emergency phone number clearly by your phone.
- Post the number of the ASPCA's Poison Control Center (888-426-4435) by your phone.
- Keep a special box of first-aid supplies for your dog so that you'll have everything you need (www.canismajor.com/dog/fstaidk.html).

Quickly calling for help and tending to the emergency are huge time savers. The other thing you'll need to do is stay calm.

Chapter 4

Housetraining Your Puppy

Teaching your puppy where you want him to eliminate and then reinforcing that message is a top priority. Cuteness fades fast when your angelic bundle goes lumbering off to your living room, and before you can say "No," squats and pees on your most expensive carpet. Lesson learned: Don't trust the little one to be able to hold it or to reliably understand what you want him to do for several weeks—or even months.

Quick Tip

Make your puppy's crate an inviting place by putting a couple of soft, old towels down inside it, as well as some safe toys.

Puppies don't understand that we want them to eliminate outside. In fact, they aren't even conscious of needing to eliminate. For them, when nature calls, they simply respond and go. Puppies need to be trained to eliminate where we want them to go, whether it's outside, or if you own a toy breed and live in an apartment in a city, a litter box or particular corner.

SUCCESSFUL HOUSETRAINING

Successful housetraining begins with a schedule and boundaries. The schedule is important because it lets you (and your puppy, eventually) know what to expect. Puppy eats, puppy needs to eliminate. Puppy plays, puppy needs to eliminate. Puppy naps, puppy needs to eliminate. You take him out when he needs to go, he does his business—success! (See Chapter 1 for a sample of a typical schedule.)

Boundaries help to prevent accidents by confining your puppy to an area he shouldn't want to soil because he also sleeps there, and to a place that's easier for you to clean. The ideal boundaries are established by a crate, although a puppy-proofed room like a kitchen or mudroom secured with a baby gate also can do the job.

WHY A CRATE IS GREAT

A crate was on the list of basic puppy supplies in Chapter 1, and quicker success with housetraining is the primary reason (although there are others). How does it work? A properly outfitted crate will serve as your puppy's own "den," a place where he will sleep, play, and possibly eat—not a place he'll want to soil. Crates are designed to safely contain puppies and dogs. They're constructed of chew-proof sides that are adequately ventilated, the latch is secure, and they are easy to clean. As we discussed in Chapter 1, your puppy should have room to stand up, turn around, and stretch out, but not so much room he can eliminate on the other side.

CRATE "DON'TS"

A crate is not a puppy prison. You should never put your puppy in the crate in anger and "lock the door" to leave him there. Never leave him in the crate for longer than a few hours at a time and in the beginning for no more than a half hour or so. If you abuse your puppy this way, he will not see the crate as a den but instead as a very frightening place, and he will protest being confined to it by howling and trying to chew it apart, which could cause serious injury.

GETTING USED TO THE CRATE

As beneficial as the crate can be, you can't expect your pup to simply take to it right away. He will need to be made to feel comfortable and safe there. Put a soft towel or blanket in the crate right away—something easy to wash in case of an accident. Put one especially intriguing toy in the back of the crate.

Place the crate in an area where your family spends a lot of time, like the kitchen or family room. Again, the crate shouldn't represent solitary confinement to the puppy—it should be a safe haven.

When introducing your puppy to the crate, leave the door open, and with a handful of treats, kneel down beside the crate with him. Toss a treat into the back of the crate. Your puppy should go in to get it. Praise him for going in and out easily. Do this a few times. Then, as he goes in after a treat, quietly close the door. When he turns to come back out, pause a minute before opening the door. If he starts to cry, don't respond in any way, and avoid eye contact. He'll eventually pause, and this is when you should pop the door and let him out. You want him to learn that being quiet is his cue to freedom, not crying.

USING THE CRATE TO HOUSETRAIN

Once your pup knows his crate is a good place, begin

Make It Easy: Crate Training

Follow these suggestions, and your crate training should advance smoothly.

- **Spend about ten minutes twice a day the first couple of days just introducing your puppy to the crate.**
- **Feed him a couple of meals in the crate.**
- **As he gets used to it, keep the door closed for longer and longer periods of time.**
- **Keep a highly desirable chew toy, like a Nylabone, in the crate so that he has something to play with.**
- **Play classical or easy listening music (quietly) to help to calm him.**
- **Don't let him out when he's fussing, only when he's quiet.**

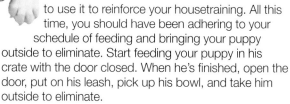

to use it to reinforce your housetraining. All this time, you should have been adhering to your schedule of feeding and bringing your puppy outside to eliminate. Start feeding your puppy in his crate with the door closed. When he's finished, open the door, put on his leash, pick up his bowl, and take him outside to eliminate.

Start incorporating crate time into the rest of your day, too. After eliminating and playing for a bit, put him in his crate for a little while. Always take him to eliminate immediately when letting him out of the crate. He'll learn that a potty break happens when he's let out, which is a cue to hold it.

BEDTIME HOUSETRAINING

A rigorous schedule demands a couple of trips outside after the puppy's final meal and one just before retiring for the night. If you're crate training your pup, you can move his crate upstairs to the bedroom with you or have a separate one there. When you put him in the crate for the night, close the door (even on the first night), but be sure that he can see you, and don't respond when he cries.

If you aren't using a crate, set up the puppy's bed in a place where he can see you, and tie the end of his leash onto something solid nearby. There should be enough slack in the lead so that he can get up and down and move around, but not so much that he can pace, paw at your bed, or move around too much. You want the leash to serve as his "boundary" to keep him in bed. Information on coping with puppy's first night is in Chapter 1.

ELIMINATING ON CUE

Believe it or not, it's not enough that your puppy goes when you take him outside (although it's a lot better than an accident inside!). Ideally, you want your puppy to understand that he should eliminate in a particular spot, and that he should eliminate on cue. Sound like too much to hope for? It's actually very achievable because it's something you can "train" every single time you go out—and that's often.

THE SPOT AND THE CUE

From day one, based on the schedule you've established, put your puppy's leash on and take him outside. Have a baggie of treats ready by his leash for every outing, and bring it with you.

Take him to the place where you want him to eliminate, and stay there with him. If he goes, great! Make a big deal out of it. Choose a word that you want him to associate with eliminating, like "potty," and praise him enthusiastically. Don't worry about going overboard or looking silly—you want him to know that he has just made you very happy. Say "Good potty!" and give him a treat, some petting, and more praise; if he's pooped, too, take him for a walk.

You can teach your puppy to eliminate on cue.

DON'T LET HIM TRAIN YOU

You want your puppy to pee and poop around the same spot, and you want him to do both fairly soon when you get outside. If he does, he gets extra time outside. If he doesn't, back inside

Don't let your puppy take control of his time outside—you decide when he can play after he's relieved himself.

until it's time—which may be immediately. What you *don't* want to do is to establish a routine where you go out and you need to take him for a ten-minute walk before he'll even think about pooping. He may begin to do this if you bring him back inside too quickly. Dogs love being outside and sniffing around, and if you simply whisk your puppy in and out when it's potty time, he'll figure out that he needs to stall you somehow.

ACCIDENTS WILL HAPPEN

No matter how diligent you are and no matter how quickly your puppy seems to be catching on, there will be times when he pees or poops in the house. Remember, he's just a baby, and even if he does it just after you've come in from a successful elimination and walk, he's not doing it to spite or upset you. This doesn't mean that he should get the idea that you're not upset by his behavior, but be patient and keep your perspective.

If you are right there when your puppy begins to eliminate, say "NO" sharply, and scoop him up to get him outside. Picking him up will usually halt the flow. If it doesn't, hold him out in front of you as you head for the door. Carry him to his spot and say "Potty." He may not need to go anymore, or he may be frightened and reluctant. Give him a minute or so, then take him inside and confine him to his crate or tie his lead to something stable so that he can't move too far.

Get the paper towels and the urine odor eliminator (Nature's Miracle is one such product), and with him in sight, say "Naughty puppy. This is naughty" as you clean up the mess. Speak with displeasure, but direct your scolding not to the puppy but to the accident. Throw the mess away, and take your puppy to his spot again, just in case. Do not be angry with your puppy. All you're teaching him by yelling at him is that you can be scary.

If you find an accident in the house, simply resign yourself to cleaning it up the best you can and to better confining your puppy and/or taking him out more often. Do not drag him to the spot, rub his nose in it, yell at him, drag him outside, or anything else punitive. Once he's done his thing, he's on to something else. He will not understand why you're upset; he'll simply learn that you can be an ogre and that it may be wiser to avoid you. It's your responsibility to help him succeed, not to punish him when he's made a mistake.

A MUST-HAVE FOR DOG OWNERS

If you think that your puppy is the only one having accidents, go to the pet supply store and see how many products there are to assist with and clean up doggy messes. A product you won't want to be without is a bottle of urine odor eliminator. It's an enzyme formula that removes the smell and odor of urine and other tough messes like vomit and diarrhea. Besides doing the best possible job to get rid of the accident, this product also won't leave the spot smelling like a doggy toilet, which often encourages repeat accidents. Choose the product you think will work best for you, and follow the instructions.

Did You Know?

An "ex-pen" is like a doggy playpen. It's designed to be a temporary confinement system for your pup so that he can't get into too much trouble. They can be set up inside or outside.

Accidents happen—don't punish your puppy for housetraining mistakes.

Quick
&Easy

Chapter 5

Teaching Puppy Manners

Don't think of training as imposing your will over his, showing him who's boss, or any of the other dominance-oriented ideas you may have. Instead, think of training as the language you will share so that he knows what it is you want him to do. Using your language, you may think that you're telling your puppy to sit, to down, or to come, but unless you teach him what those words mean, he can't know—he doesn't speak your language. He's not purposely "not listening" or disobeying when you tell him something and he doesn't do it—he's simply not understanding. Teaching him the meanings of your words takes "the three Ps": patience, practice, and praise.

TIME TO TRAIN

Years ago, dog training was based on punishment, such as jerking the leash, to let a dog know when he'd done something wrong. Nowadays, dog trainers and behaviorists have developed positive training methods, which include lure-reward training using treats, clickers, voice, and other cues to elicit desired behavior. By making training positive, your puppy will be eager to learn new things, and the bond between you will remain strong.

TOOLS

Here's what you'll need to train your puppy:
- collar
- leash
- training treats, such as a small chunk of cheese, cooked meat, hotdog, piece of popcorn— something irresistible to your puppy
- a distraction-free area
- a few minutes a day

BASIC LESSONS

Sit, stay, down, come, and *walk quietly,* are the lessons we're going to begin with because they form the foundation for good household manners.

TEACHING *SIT*

You're going to love teaching this command— it's so easy! With your puppy in his collar and in a fairly confined space that's relatively distraction-free, get a really tasty treat and let your puppy know that you have something super yummy. Tease him a little bit with the treat so that his full attention is on you.

When he is fully focused on you and the treat, and he is directly in front of you, bring the treat to his nose. Then, as he's working to get at it with his mouth, slowly lift it up between his eyes and above his head. Don't say anything as you're luring him through this. As his face moves up to follow the treat, his bottom will drop and he'll naturally sit. As soon as his bottom hits the ground, give him the treat and say "Good sit!" Do this two or three times in a row—not more than that—

Keep training sessions short—end them while your puppy is still interested.

and do it several times a day.

If your pup starts to back up instead of dropping his bottom as you lift the treat, position him so that he will back up into a cupboard or wall and will need to sit. As you practice teaching *sit*, move away from the wall.

TEACHING *STAY*

Stay is one of the next commands you should teach.

With your pup in his happy *sit*, open your hand with the palm facing his face, and say (like you mean it) "Stay." Say it firmly but gently. Don't drag it out, don't say it thinking it'll never work—just say "Stay." Count slowly to two, say "Good stay!" and give him a treat when you say "Good stay!" That's it—just a couple of seconds at first.

Raise a treat above your pup's head to get him to sit.

A great time to practice *stay* is just before meals. If you've been working on *sit* all along, he should almost be doing that automatically when mealtime comes around. Now, with him in a *sit*, as you're going to put the bowl down, stop, say "Stay," and hold the bowl for two counts. Then put bowl on the floor with a "Good stay!" and "Good boy!"

TEACHING *DOWN*

Down isn't as easy to teach—or learn—as *sit* and even *stay*, so be patient. Going down at your request demonstrates real trust on the part of your puppy. Earn it, don't force it.

With the tastiest of treats to entice him, lure your puppy to you and ask him to sit. He should be happy to do that. Praise him when he does, but don't offer him the treat just yet. Kneel down in front of him (ask him to sit again if necessary), and hold the treat at his nose so that he is really motivated by it. Slowly move the treat down toward the floor and out toward you. You want him to

Make It Easy: Sit

Here's how to teach sit as easy as 1-2-3.

- Use a tasty treat to attract and lure your puppy.
- Hold the treat near his nose, and slowly lift it up between his eyes and above his head.
- When his bottom hits the floor (as his head goes up), say "Good sit!" and give the treat.

Down can be difficult for a puppy to learn, so go slowly and be patient.

bring his head down and then start moving his paws out so his elbows land on the floor. As soon as they do, give the treat with an encouraging "Good down."

Some puppies will stand up as their noses go down to retrieve the treat near the floor. Guard against this response by bringing the treat down slowly so that he wants to stay in a sitting/squatting position. Bring the treat toward you from slightly off the floor, and if you need to, help position the pup with your hands as you lure/reward him.

Always work the *down* from the *sit* position first. Once he's down and has been rewarded, release him with an "Okay" so that he gets the idea that *down* only means all the way on the floor and not to the floor and then back up.

TEACHING *COME*

Come can be difficult for easily distractable puppies. Set yourself up to succeed easily from the very beginning. Work in a room with no distractions and with your puppy in his collar with the leash attached. Armed with some tasty treats, simply watch your puppy for a couple minutes. When he becomes interested in something other than you, say "Puppy [his name], come" in a high, happy voice, and offer the treat. As he approaches, give him the treat and say "Good come." Do this a few times, then take off the leash and end the training session.

Practice calling your puppy to come to you in as many ways as possible. When you let him out of his crate or confined space, call and reward him for coming to you. When you're going to get his leash to take him for a potty break/walk, call and reward him for coming to you. At mealtime, use some of his kibble to call him to you, rewarding him with some from your hand when he does.

For the first week or so, keep the distance he has to travel to get to you short so that he can't become distracted. The lesson is that when you call, he comes, he gets a treat and a hug, and then he can go do something else. When he's coming to you this way 99.9 percent of the time, start lengthening the distances from which you call him.

As your puppy grows and keeps responding to his name and the *come* command, begin working with him on a longer leash. Always call "Puppy, come" just once. If you don't get a response, turn away from him and start walking, even if you need to pull him to move him in your direction. As he's moving toward you, repeat the request and bring him in to you by holding out the treat.

TEACHING *WALK QUIETLY*

You should teach your puppy that you want him to walk quietly with you without pulling, lunging, or sitting and not moving.

When it's time to go outside, ask your puppy to sit while you put on his collar and leash. It's harder to squirm and shimmy about when you're sitting. If he gets up while you're putting on the collar, stop and ask him again to sit. He should sit politely while you're outfitting him for his walk. That means sitting while you put the leash on, too.

With his collar and leash on, give the release command "Okay," and head for the door. At the door, ask him to sit while you open the door. Only open it if he's sitting. This will be hard for both of you at first, but it's a great habit to get into, and it teaches your puppy to sit at the door and wait for what he wants.

Once out the door, ask him to sit again as you close and lock the door. Your puppy only gets to go when he's done what you ask. This is how you're going to start

Quick Tip

To keep your lessons fun and successful, don't ask for too much of a stay from your young pup. A few seconds is wonderful!

When teaching come, keep the distance your pup has to travel to you short.

Quick Tip

If you want your puppy to come to you any time you call (and that should be your goal), he needs to know that 100 percent of the time you call you will shower him with something he loves. Lucky for you, it's easy to do that—treats, toys, praise, a game of tug, belly rubs, sitting in your lap—are all things any puppy would come for.

going on your walks.

At any time during the walk, ask your pup to sit. If he does, give him a treat and a hearty "Good sit" and immediately start walking again. If he doesn't, stop walking and stand still. When his attention is back on you, ask again. Don't say "Sit....sit....[Fido], sit...Sit! SIT!" This teaches him that you don't really mean it the first time you ask. Simply do nothing until he complies. He sits, you move.

If he's interested in going anywhere, eventually he'll learn that you're in charge of whether and how far he's going to go. If he pulls, simply stop dead in your tracks until he doubles back and looks to you for an answer. Ask him to sit, and if he does, reward and move on. You are going to feel silly and awkward doing this, but it will pay off in the end. Patience, practice, and praise!

THE IMPORTANCE OF SOCIALIZATION

What if you lived with a family that never went out and did anything with other people? Yours was a loving family, and everyone was happy, but you didn't go to school with other kids, you didn't go to the movies, you didn't play sports—you basically lived in a bubble. How scary it would be for you to eventually run into other people—loud people, rough people, old people, all different types? What if all of a sudden a bunch of them came to your house? Would you hide, run away, try to protect your family?

It's an unimaginable scenario for most of us, but that's what it's like for a puppy who's growing into a dog and living with a family that never exposes him to other people and animals. Your puppy is friendly and nice with you because he trusts you. Why should he trust people or other dogs he doesn't know? Most puppies and dogs don't automatically trust strangers. They are as apprehensive as we would be.

For the emotional health and physical safety of your pup and for the safety of your family, it is critical to get him out into the world where he can meet and greet as many kinds of people, other animals, and environments as possible. Every positive interaction will boost his self-confidence and make him less afraid. It will expose him to safe and unsafe situations where you will be there to assure or to rescue him so that he can better handle all other experiences.

Because puppies are individuals and are each sensitive in their own ways, you need to be a real protector and leader. Don't put your puppy in danger by encouraging him to "sniff" another dog who seems aggressive; don't let a group of kids have their way with your puppy; don't turn him loose in a dog run before taking a look at the other dogs to make sure that they're not too boisterous for your young one. Use common sense and your own sensitivity to expose him in as positive and beneficial a way as possible. Check into enrolling in a puppy kindergarten class, where your pup will have the chance to play with other pups and get some early training under the supervision of a professional trainer. To make meetings with strangers positive, have a supply of treats with you and allow the other person to offer them to your pup.

Socialization with other puppies, dogs, children, and people is essential for a well-adjusted dog.

Quick
&Easy

Chapter 6

Puppy Problem Solving

Is your puppy misbehaving? You'll need to do the following things immediately, to get him on the road to good behavior:

- Set limits.
- Reward only for good behavior.
- Don't respond emotionally.

Don't respond to bad behavior; reward behavior you do want from your puppy.

SETTING LIMITS

What are some ways to set limits? Establish house rules and stick to them. Your puppy does not make the rules. Limit him to a crate or a small room set off with a baby gate. When it's necessary to leave the crate or room, put a leash on him and supervise him at all times. No more running through the house when he wants to. Limit his comings and goings to necessary trips: to the potty, to eat, or for short periods of play.

Limit the number of people he can play with at any one time, and keep play as quiet as possible. Limit the length of your walks. Limit allowing him on any furniture until he's earned it. Revisit the schedule discussed in Chapter 1, and if necessary, revise and hone it so that your puppy's time is accounted for and is under your control. This doesn't need to be forever, but it will need to be until he learns what's acceptable.

REWARD ONLY FOR GOOD BEHAVIOR

Don't respond to bad behavior by yelling and screaming. Instead, when your puppy does something you dislike, stop what you're doing and put him in his confined area so that he is not receiving any input from you. This may make the situation worse before it gets better because your puppy will protest. But be strong, and only reward the behavior you want (a quiet puppy, a pup who sits when asked, etc.). Your attention and a tasty treat at the right time should get the message across, but this is something that takes time!

DON'T RESPOND EMOTIONALLY

Not responding emotionally is so hard—it goes against

every instinct we have. However, the less you do it, the less attention you're giving your puppy, good or bad. You should show your puppy positive emotions when he does something you want or like (that's easy!) and negative emotions only when you want to warn your puppy, as in a sharp, stern "NO!" Once you've gotten a response, deal with the situation and put your emotions on hold.

RECURRING PROBLEMS

If you start following the three suggestions outlined in the beginning of the chapter and adhere to them diligently, you should see typical problems begin to solve themselves. Remember, though, that puppies are puppies. They are living beings who have needs. Don't misinterpret some bad behaviors as simple responses to too few limits or the need for attention. Some behaviors are rooted in physical problems that may or may not be obvious. If you have a recurring problem that seems to defy your best efforts, speak to your veterinarian about it.

Quick Tip

Just like kids, puppies crave attention, and they're not selective about whether it's positive or negative attention. Yelling and scolding, while scary, is still attention.

Barking is a natural behavior for dogs, but you can teach your puppy to "quiet" when he gets out of control.

COMMON PUPPY PROBLEMS

Here's a quick list of eight common puppy problems:

1. barking or whining
2. begging
3. chewing
4. digging
5. jumping up
6. mouthing and nipping
7. stealing food, clothes, or other objects
8. submissive urination

BARKING OR WHINING

First thing to remember is not to "bark" or whine back, which you're doing if you yell at or plead with your puppy while he's vocalizing this way. The message he gets from you "barking back" is that maybe he should be louder, or maybe he should repeat himself so that you stop. Instead, teach him to bark on command with the word *speak*, or *bark*, and to be quiet on command with the word *shush* or *quiet*. It's usually easier to teach *speak* first when your pup is actually barking. Simply encourage him by saying "Good speak." Feeding him will necessitate that he stop barking to chew and swallow. When he is finally quiet, say "Good shush," and reward him again.

Make It Easy: No Begging

To discourage your pup from begging while you're eating, keep these things in mind:

- **Confine him when it's your turn to eat.**
- **If you want to give leftovers, save them and incorporate them into his regular meal, or feed them as a snack when your meal is cleaned up.**
- **Tell guests not to feed your pup from the table while snacking or at a barbecue, etc.**

BEGGING

This is an easier bad habit to prevent than to cure, so from the very beginning, when it's time for you to eat, put your pup in his crate or a confined room with an engaging chew toy to occupy him. Only let him out when you're finished, and if you want to feed him leftovers, put them in his food bowl and incorporate them into regular meals.

If you have a beggar, start crating or confining him, and steel yourself and your family to suffer through the barking and whining for as long as it takes. Only release him from the confinement when he is quiet.

CHEWING

Puppies need to chew. Accept this fact and take on the responsibility of providing him with safe, acceptable chew toys, like Nylabones. If he's chewing stuff around the house, don't let him loose in the house. Crating or confining him with the chews you've selected will leave him with little choice but to satisfy his needs with those. If he simply won't take to something you think is safe and acceptable, keep trying until you find something he likes. Again, your veterinarian or trainer is a good resource for suggestions.

DIGGING

If you have a pup who loves to dig—and digging is a natural canine instinct and can't be completely shut down—don't fight him, join him! Select a spot in your yard or on your walk where he won't do too much damage if he digs. Encourage him to use that spot by burying something there that he needs to dig out, and praise him when he does. Set up a small sandbox in your yard where your puppy can dig. If he's digging in an unacceptable spot, it's because you're not supervising him or directing him to an acceptable spot.

The same is true for "digging" indoors. If your pup is scratching at the floor, he's probably anxious or bored. He may well be somewhere he's not supposed to be. Put him someplace safe (confined), and give him toys and chews to play with. Take him outside or for a walk, and direct him to his digging spot.

JUMPING UP

Your puppy can't jump up on someone if he's sitting down, lying down, or otherwise confined. Work on this problem with a friend or neighbor as well as other family members. Put your puppy on leash, have someone (who is holding some treats) ring the doorbell, approach with your puppy, and ask him to sit. If he sits, open the door. If he doesn't sit, wait until he does. When the person comes in, have her ask the pup to sit. If he sits, he gets a treat. If he doesn't sit, the person should turn her back on the pup for a moment. Make sure that your puppy doesn't jump up on her by holding on to his leash. Ask him to sit first, and be sure he does. Then the person should turn around and ask him to sit, too. Repeat until the puppy complies.

This is something you'll need to do over and over again until your pup can control himself. Even if you confine him

Quick Tip

While teaching your pup to sit when visitors come through the door, keep a jar of small training snacks by the door so that you can give your guest a few to use as rewards. Make sure that the jar has a tight-fitting lid for when you're not using it.

If your pup jumps up, teach him an alternate behavior, like *sit*.

Select a spot in your yard where it's okay for your pup to dig.

when you're expecting guests, eventually you'll want to include him in the gathering, in which case he'll need to know how to properly greet the guests—by sitting and being rewarded for it. How great is that?

MOUTHING AND NIPPING

A puppy's mouth is akin to a baby's hands—a primary source for investigating everything in the world around him. He will come at you and your kids with his mouth because he wants to investigate and play, and that's what he did with his littermates. Learning when he's been too rough is part of his necessary development. His mom let him know, and his littermates did, too. How can you?

When your puppy clamps down a bit too hard with those razor-sharp puppy teeth, don't pull away, which will instinctively cause him to want to hold tighter. Instead, cry out in pain as a puppy would, by whimpering. This should surprise him enough to stop and look up at you. As soon as he stops, slowly move your hand/body away, and direct his mouth to something he can chew on, preferably an acceptable toy, although you may have to improvise at the moment. If he comes at you again, stop interacting with him. Confining or crating him is like giving your baby a "time-out."

Teach your kids how to respond to your puppy, too, because they are more inclined to

Quick Tip

If you have a child or children who become too upset by the puppy's mouthing, supervise all their interactions so that you can step in and redirect the play, removing your puppy if necessary.

get upset and pull away, which often leads to wrestling and flailing that can seriously hurt everyone.

SEPARATION ANXIETY

Separation anxiety is what some veterinarians and trainers refer to when a puppy or dog goes nuts when his family leaves him alone, attempting to destroy his surroundings, barking and crying uncontrollably, and otherwise causing havoc when left alone. The result is not pleasant for you and is not good for your puppy.

To combat this reaction, acclimate your pup to your comings and goings by starting small and making the experience a positive one. Without making a big fuss, decide to leave the house. Put your pup in his crate or room with a favorite chew toy, turn the radio on to a classical or soft rock station (something soothing), and without saying another word, pick up your coat, bag, and car keys, and leave the house.

A serious case of separation anxiety might need the help of a trainer or behaviorist.

Walk around the house quietly, listening to or spying on your pup without him knowing. Give him a couple of minutes, depending on whether he gets upset when you leave or not. If he does, allow him to settle down (a really appealing chew toy should be enough—if it's not, find something more appealing). If he doesn't, great.

When he's quiet and you've been out more than five minutes, come back in as if nothing has happened, put your things down, and quietly and calmly greet your pup. Do not run to him and smother him with kisses. Put on his leash and bring him outside, just as you would if you were returning from a longer trip. Let him learn that you come home and take care of his needs.

Do this a few times a day in the first days and weeks you have your pup, increasing the amount of time you are gone from the house. Stack the odds in your favor by making sure that your pup has something worth playing with, that the radio is loud enough but not too loud, that there is sufficient light and heat, and that you have made sure that he's comfortable and safe. If you're confining him to a room, puppy-proof it thoroughly.

Did You Know?

Puppies who have not been adequately socialized may confuse small children with prey—all the more reason to expose your pup to all kinds of kids!

STEALING FOOD, CLOTHING, OR OTHER OBJECTS

Fortunately, stealing is a fairly easy problem to solve because your puppy can't steal what he can't get to. Unfortunately, the onus is really on you. You need to be perpetually on the lookout for what could be considered fair game: accessible garbage cans, food left anywhere within reach, open closet doors, etc. Make the inappropriate objects of his desire inaccessible while at the same time being sure to provide plenty of appropriate chews and other toys. Play with your dog with those toys so that the pleasure for him is in using them only.

When he does steal, don't start chasing him, or you're initiating a game. Call him to you or go after him methodically and unemotionally until you can hold him. Tell him "Leave it" as you open his mouth to remove the object. Be careful while doing this; if you sense that your puppy is getting overly aggressive, leave him. Confine him at the earliest opportunity, and commit to working with an experienced dog trainer or behaviorist. The last thing you want is a puppy to turn on you over a stolen object.

SUBMISSIVE URINATION

When you come inside to greet your puppy, does he flop down and begin to wet himself? If so, you have a submissive urinator. First, visit your vet to be sure that the problem isn't due to a health issue. If it's not, keep your puppy somewhere that's easy to clean so that you're not doubly frustrated by a soiled carpet.

With your pup crated or in a safe, confined space, when you approach to greet him after being away for a bit, do so in as emotionless a way as possible. If the problem has been going on for a while, you probably approach him reluctantly, anxiously, or even suspiciously. He can pick up on your feelings, and they can contribute to his own anxiousness. Pretend he's a strange dog who you need to calmly and gently get out the door as quickly as possible so that he can do his business outside.

If he urinates as you're going outside, don't react.

Make sure that your puppy is getting enough attention and exercise—a tired pup is a good pup!

Stay the course to the outside, let him do his thing, confine him again while you clean up, and then get on with the rest of your day. You will need to respond as unemotionally as possible until you feel that you're making progress. Slow and steady is the key.

A LAST THOUGHT ON PROBLEMS

Like any new venture, owning a puppy is going to challenge you in ways you never thought possible. There will be times you wonder how anyone can love a dog. When you have these thoughts, or you're facing issues that seem too big for you to handle, seek help. Professionals are professionals for a reason: They know how to solve the problems of their profession. A dog trainer you trust and can work with may be just the solution, and she will be happy to help. Find one near you through the Association of Pet Dog Trainers (APDT), an organization with many certified members. They're at www.apdt. com, or call 1-800-PET-DOGS. Don't let your pup become another sad statistic of an abandoned dog. You both deserve better.

Quick Tip

Storing your garbage can behind a door that can be closed securely will eliminate the problem of your pup getting into the garbage.

Well-Behaved Puppy

Note: **Boldfaced** numbers indicate illustrations; an italic *t* indicates tables.

PHOTO CREDITS

Jacqueline Abromeit (Shutterstock): 4-5
Annette (Shutterstock): 14
Anyka (Shutterstock): 57
Casey K. Bishop (Shutterstock): 16-17
Scott Bolster (Shutterstock): 1
Katrina Brown (Shutterstock): 23
Denise Campione (Shutterstock): 27 (top)
Lars Christensen (Shutterstock): 24
Condor 36 (Shutterstock): 61
Waldemar Dabrowski (Shutterstock): 44-45, 51, 60
Tad Denson (Shutterstock): 43, 59
Isabelle Francais: 7 (bottom), 18, 19, 25, 26, 30, 31, 39, 41, 42, 48, 49, 55
Eric Geveart (Shutterstock): 6
GJS (Shutterstock): 58
Interpet: 47 (top)
Eric Isselee (Shutterstock): 3, 9, 12, 13, 40, 47 (bottom), 54
Jim Larson (Shutterstock): 36-37
Shirelle Reggio Manning: 21
Sean Nel (Shutterstock): 8
Steven Pepple (Shutterstock): 34
Pieter (Shutterstock): 46
Pixshots (Shutterstock): 52-53
Rick's Photography (Shutterstock): 20
Elena Sherengovskaya (Shutterstock): 27 (bottom)
Magdalena Szachowska (Shutterstock): 35
Ferenc Szelepcsenyi (Shutterstock): 56
Tootles (Shutterstock): 28-29
Lynn Watson (Shutterstock): 10
Jan de Wild (Shutterstock): 32

ABOUT THE AUTHOR

Dominique De Vito has been involved in pet publishing for over 10 years, and has helped create many award-winning books. A member of the Association of Pet Dog Trainers and the Dog Writers Association of America, she is the author of *Training Your Dog* for the Animal Planet™ Pet Care Library. She is currently a freelance editor and writer who lives with her husband, two dogs, and twin boys in New Jersey and New York state.

NATURAL with added VITAMINS

Nutri Dent®
MD

Promotes Optimal Dental Health!

360° Design
Cleaning Action!

Dogs Love'em!™

AVAILABLE IN MULTIPLE SIZES AND FLAVORS.

Nylabone®

Trusted For Over 40 Years

MADE IN THE USA

Our Mission with Nutri Dent® is to promote optimal dental health for dogs through a trusted, natural, delicious chew that provides effective cleaning action...GUARANTEED to make your dog go wild with anticipation and happiness!!!

Nylabone Products • P.O. Box 427, Neptune, NJ 07754-0427 • 1-800-631-2188 • Fax: 732-988-5466
www.nylabone.com • info@nylabone.com • For more information contact your sales representative or contact us at sales@tfh.com   A275